TABLE OF CONTENTS

Introduction

Chapter One: What Is Your Dream?   7

Chapter Two: Discipline   10

Chapter Three: Relationships   14

Chapter Four: Execution   18

Chapter Five: Attitude   21

Chapter Six: Motivation   24

Chapter Seven: Sacrifice   28

Conclusion   30

It Was All a Dream is a wonderful book about 11 men who dreamed outside of themselves while on the campus of one of America's greatest historically black colleges, Alabama State University. As an alumna of ASU, I saw the tenacious spirit firsthand from many of these young men. It was just as evident then that they wanted to help and to inspire the younger generation to greatness. This is a great read for all future leaders and serves as a great example of what ASU and other historically black colleges and universities can produce. I salute TallaDallas in all endeavors.

Judge Shera Grant
District Court Judge
1999 graduate, Alabama State University

Any young person interested in overcoming adversities and dreaming big dreams should unequivocally associate with the men of TDI as described in this book. For over 20 years, I have witnessed the maturation of this group of men into productive contributors to society. They are a glowing example of the power of prayer and persistence in the lives of young African American males.

Vergil Chames, III
Former Student Affairs Administrator, Alabama State University
Venture Capitalist, River Region Capital

For the past 20 years, I have had the opportunity to help provide access to thousands of students looking to gain higher education and to improve their lives. During this time, I have had the opportunity to help students in foster care looking for a way out and others who had attended some of the most prestigious private schools on their way to the Ivy League. No matter what the background of the students, they all have one common characteristic: how to reach that next level. This book serves as more than motivation to get through college but as a guide to get through the uncertain road to adulthood through the eyes of 11 men who have experienced many of the peaks and valleys of life on the way to achieving their individual dreams. Through their experiences and friendship, the men of TDI have created a tool that can serve as an inspiration to us all to aid in reaching our full potential.

Timothy L. Fields
Associate Dean, Emory University
1998 graduate, Morehouse University

Young African American males are suffering from a lack of guidance in the community. It is important that we mentor them to show our youth that there is more to life than the streets. Mentorship molded me into the man I am today. Without it, I would still have doubts about what I can accomplish. The guidance I had as a youth opened my eyes to something far bigger than myself. They taught me not to be a cancer to society but to be a contributor to it. That is why organizations like TDI are important.

Joey Scott
Olympic Developmental Coach
Three-time Olympic Track and Field Coach
Four-time World Championships Coach
Coached many top-10 ranked youth athletes

ABOUT TDI

In the fall of 1993, a group of over ten young men from Talladega, Alabama, and Dallas, Texas, met as freshmen on the campus of Alabama State University. They started what is now a life-long friendship with a common ambition to be successful and a desire to use their knowledge, time, and monetary gifts to give back through an organization they founded called TallaDallas, now operating as TDI.

MISSION STATEMENT

TDI's mission is dedicated to assisting people to turn their dreams into reality by providing scholarships, mentoring, and professional development. Through our story and brand, we will help by developing or enhancing leadership qualities, equipping people with tools for professional growth, or coaching habits for success.

VISION STATEMENT

Our vision is to advance human well-being by assisting in developing holistic, well-rounded individuals who will become positive contributors to society and will in turn assist in reciprocating that effort for future generations of young men and women.

SLOGAN

Turning Dreams Into Realities

D.R.E.A.M.S. SEMINAR

Over the past few years, we have been presenting our flagship seminar called the D.R.E.A.M.S. Seminar. This seminar is a summary of the various principles that we have learned over our lives that have been keys to our success in achieving our dreams as a group. Of course, these aren't the only tools that have been beneficial to us, but they are ones that we could collectively see in our individual stories that you saw in the book.

We enjoy reading leadership books such as *21 Laws of Leadership* by John Maxwell and *StrengthsFinder 2.0* by Tom Rath. We incorporate some of their principles into our lives as we lead corporations, ministries, and our own businesses. But we believe that if you have a dream or a vision for your life and if you apply these principles, then you will be able to turn those dreams into realities.

The feedback that we have received from students just like you in various states is the reason we decided to create this workbook and make it available. This workbook will allow you to work on individual principles and see how you can apply them to your life.

The six TDI principles that make up the seminar are:

D–Discipline
R–Relationships
E–Execution
A–Attitude
M–Motivation
S–Sacrifice

INTRODUCTION

On July 26, 2016, we released our book, *It Was All a Dream*, which is a chronicle of the lives of 11 African American men from the South who had dreams of becoming successful and changing the way we were perceived because of the color of our skin or the college we attended. Now we are focused on giving back to young people all over the country through our nonprofit organization, Turning Dreams Into Realities, Inc. (TDI). We share an appreciation for education, relationships, fun, family, success, music, and most importantly a dedication to our dreams. What is the key to our success? Our D.R.E.A.M.S. (Discipline, Relationships, Execution, Attitude, Motivation, and Sacrifice).

In his chapter of the book, "Stereotypes of a Black Man Misunderstood," co-author Dr. Anthony Lewis writes, "Research states that a single-parent family background and the poverty that usually accompanies it render children twice as likely to drop out of high school, 2.5 times as likely to become out-of-wedlock teen parents, and 1.4 times as likely to be unemployed. These children miss more days of school, have lower educational aspirations, receive lower grades, and eventually divorce more often as adults. They are almost twice as likely to exhibit antisocial behavior as adults; 25 to 50 percent more likely to manifest such behavioral problems as anxiety, depression, hyperactivity, or dependence; two to three times more likely to need psychiatric care; and much more likely to commit suicide as teenagers."

Just like the late, great rapper Biggie Smalls alluded to in his classic hit "Juicy," he went from negative to positive, changed from a common thief to a successful entertainer, broke the stereotypes of what black men could aspire to be, and learned to live life without fear. Smalls credited all his success to his ability to dream. His lyrics inspired our own dreams, and this workbook was developed with young people in mind. If you have a dream and simply need help turning that dream into a reality, then this resource will help you. For more information, please visit us at www.tdi2r.org.

HOW TO USE THIS WORKBOOK

Our goal for creating this resource was to help community organizations, churches, schools, and other mentor groups that are looking for real-life applications to help young people identify ways to see the journey of life through a broader lens. Our goal is to help young leadership and transform their dreams into realities. We have developed a TDI mentorship program that gives organizations a road map of how to follow our blueprint of developing a year-long program for young men ages 11-18. (Consultation for implementation and TDI mentor blueprint is available by emailing us at info@tdi2r.org.)

This workbook is structured with the young person in mind, and our book, *It Was All a Dream*, is the required companion and mandatory reading assignment. Each student should read the forewords, introduction, and Chapter 1 before starting the program. Then, as take-away assignments, they should read two more chapters before gathering again.

Some chapters in this workbook may build on specific chapters from the book. Each chapter in this workbook, except Chapter 1, has specific sections that give students an initial thought for the day, a key motivational quote from a great leader, two case studies for review, introspective questions to answer, instructions for how students will apply the lesson to their lives, and a weekly exposure challenge. The exposure challenge includes a reading assignment for the week, as well as a field trip suggestion or an exposure exercise that brings the lesson home for students. (The facilitator can develop this area.)

WORKBOOK

The overall goal of this workbook is to help students read about situations and stories where they can learn the D.R.E.A.M.S. principles, discuss them as a group with their facilitators and peers, and then do exposure exercises or activities that help them see the principle in action. (For example, the chapter on discipline deals with finances, so a trip to a bank to learn about checking and savings would be ideal.)

CHAPTER ONE
WHAT IS YOUR DREAM?

"It was all a dream! I used to read Word Up Magazine, Heavy D and Salt and Pepper in the limousine." Notorious B.I.G.

In his chapter, "Reach for the Stars," Marc Desgraves said, "I received little guidance about setting goals and pursuing my dreams. I didn't have a lot of motivation to excel, and I wasn't challenged and made to think of how to handle many of the situations I would face in life."

One of the reasons we wrote this workbook and our book, *It Was All a Dream*, is to help you not to suffer through that same story. We believe in you, and we want this resource to be one of the tools to challenge you to dream and to dream BIG!

What is a dream? A dream is a portrait of possibility of what you could become one day with hard work and dedication. It's like the picture on the front of a box of cake mix. Although you can see the image of a cake on the front of the box, there is no cake inside.

In order to have the cake that you see on the front of the box, you will have to look on the back to find out what type of ingredients you will need and what instructions you will have to follow to make the cake. Then you will need to combine those ingredients according to the stated instructions in order to produce the cake. The picture on the front of the box is not the cake. Rather, the picture only shows you the possibility of what you can have if you follow the instructions provided.

It's the same way with a dream. Although you may see yourself one day playing in the NBA, owning your own company, being a doctor or a lawyer, becoming president of the United States, being rich, or traveling the world, there are certain things you will have to do now in order to make that dream a reality.

In his chapter called "More Than Money," Jeremy Spratling says, "Knowing what you want to do is one thing; knowing what you don't want to do is another and is just as important. There's no shame at age 18 or 25 not knowing exactly what you want to be doing when you're 40 or 50 years old. When you're young, invest your time and energy in discovering what you love to do. Find your direction, and be true to that compass. Faith in yourself and your vision is necessary to persevere through all the small steps and hard work. Faith in yourself is also necessary to fuel the courage required to take those big leaps toward your dreams."

In this chapter, our objective is to help you to begin to take the baby steps to discover your dreams. As Jeremy said, it's no shame in not knowing now exactly what you will be doing later in life. But if you have some sense of your goals at an early age, then you have something to shoot for.

WORKBOOK

Listed below are a series of questions that may put you on the path to discovering your dreams. Consider the questions carefully, and answer them as completely as possible. There are no right or wrong answers, so write what you feel at this moment. Another key principle Jeremy stated is, "To reach your dreams, you never have to be the best in the world, just the best that you can be in the moment. You just need to live every moment to the best of your ability and continuously become the best version of yourself you can manage." That is our goal for you at this stage in your life.

Who Am I? Assessments

Strengths (What are you good at?)

Weaknesses (What aren't you good at?)

What are your best subjects in school?

What do you enjoy doing in your free time?

What are you curious about?

IT WAS ALL A DREAM

What type of job would you do for free (for example, helping people, teaching, singing, making beats)?

What makes you angry, or what bothers you (for example, abuse, not having enough money to do the things you want to do, overpriced clothes or shoes)?

If you could do one thing to change the world, what would it be?

What is your dream in life?

Now that you have some idea of who you are and what your dream is, let's explore the various principles that will help you start turning that dream into a reality.

CHAPTER TWO

DISCIPLINE

"There is no shortcut to achievement. Life requires thorough preparation."
George Washington Carver

Discipline can be defined as an activity, exercise, or a regime that develops or improves a skill through training. If you ask successful people who have achieved high levels of success, they will tell you that the number one key for them to succeed was discipline.

Discipline is what separates the good from the great, a good singer from a superstar, and an average athlete from a legend. One major area in which you are going to need to be disciplined to achieve your dream is in the area of finances. Most young people don't learn about how to properly manage money until it's too late.

In this program, we are going to teach you about budgeting, savings, and credit so that your finances won't hinder you from achieving success or make you blow your success.

CASE STUDIES
JEREMY SPRATLING, TDI MEMBER

My dream of being a business owner became my reality after a journey through many challenges and opportunities. At times, they were one and the same. Hardships are like seeds: In the right light, they can grow into wisdom and strength, but when we're lost in a dark state of mind, our hardships shrivel us with bitterness and resignation.

I am no stranger to hardship; but optimism, a vision for how I wanted to live, and faith in myself has made all the difference for me. Even though I wasn't certain what I wanted to do with my life, I had to start somewhere. I started with the suit.

I remembered a program on television about dressing for success, and the presenter said to look your most professional. Navy suits should be worn with gold buttons. I went shopping for such a suit, but I couldn't afford the right suit, so I had to find another way. At J. Riggins, I bought a plain blue suit. Then I bought a package of gold buttons at Walmart. Back in high school, I'd taken home economics, so I was able to sew on the gold buttons, and I hemmed the pants.

That Monday, I went to every bank, commercial building, and office park and applied for any available job. Because of my efforts, I landed a job as a part-time bank teller. This was the moment my business career and climb upward began, and I was happy to give notice at the restaurant where I had been working and move onward and upward.

Just as there's no such thing in life as instant success, there is also no such thing as permanent success. Success is sustained by vigilance and effort. Just because you got out of the harbor doesn't mean you can stop steering the ship. I have a plan for my sustained success and personal happiness in life, but I have to keep working the plan.

Jeremy is now the owner of CFM Services, which employs over 100 people and was recently listed as the top minority-owned business in Birmingham, Alabama.

TRENTON RICHARDSON

Trenton Richardson played football at the University of Alabama, was recognized as an All-American, and was on two BCS National Championship teams. Touted as the top running back prospect for the 2012 NFL Draft, Richardson was selected third overall by the Cleveland Browns.

Richardson and the Cleveland Browns agreed to a four-year, $20.4 million contract (fully guaranteed) with a $13.3 million signing bonus. In an interview with ESPN's *E:60*, Richardson talked about the deceit and the greed of those in his inner circle, which helped destroy his NFL career. As his career began to fall apart, his friends and family spent more than $1.6 million in less than a year.

According to Yahoo Sports, Richardson said that at the beginning of his career in Cleveland, he was giving away $10,000 at a time to friends and family so they could pay their bills. He also gave them tickets to each game. And when he had to move from Cleveland to Indianapolis, the people living in his house didn't even help him pack because they assumed he had the money to hire movers.

But in 2015, it all came crashing down. Richardson found almost 20 Netflix and Hulu accounts in his name, and he discovered charges from Amazon.com that weren't his. People were also buying bottle service at clubs by dropping his name.

"I finally just looked at my bank statements, and I was just like, 'Where did this come from? Where did that come from?' And my guy was sitting there telling me, 'Man, we was telling you.' And I know he was telling me, but that's just like telling a kid to stop running in the hall. They're going to still do it when you turn your back or you leave. It was one of those moments when I was just blinded by my heart, by loving everybody and thinking that everyone was for me. I know they love me, and I know they do care. But at the time, they took advantage of it."

Richardson said he was only spending about $300 in a two-week period. He also stated that he would never recoup much of the missing money.

"I don't even get on the internet like that. I don't even drink. Somebody had access and I probably did, but I was at big fault to that because I gave them access.... It's like how are you all spending this much money? I spend $300 in two weeks. Y'all trying to live a lifestyle that I'm not even living."

Currently, Richardson is no longer playing in the NFL. In February 2017, he was arrested on third-degree domestic violence charges in Hoover, Alabama.

WORKBOOK

KEYS TO SUCCESS
After reading the case studies, what keys did you find in Jeremy's and Trent's stories that stood out to you?

PERSONAL EVALUATION
In what areas of your life do you lack discipline. (For example, do you not set aside time to complete homework? Do you not do chores that your parents give you? Do you not eat enough fruits and vegetables?)

What is your current understanding about money?

What are your financial goals (for example, to live in a nice neighborhood, to buy your mother a house, to travel the world)?

What is a budget? Why do you need a budget?

What is the difference between income and expenses?

IT WAS ALL A DREAM

What is credit? What do you think credit is for, and why would you need it?

What is a good credit score?

How will you apply what you've learned about discipline, especially when it relates to finances, to your life?

After reading the case studies about Jeremy and Trent, what do you plan to do in the next 30 days that will help you be more disciplined? You can choose to use discipline in any area of your life, but you also must be able to connect it to your dream. Example: I plan to be more disciplined by saving some of my allowance or money that I receive for my birthday so that I can have money to use for things I want.

Dreamer's Challenge: (In this section, write down your assignment from your facilitator.)

Closing Thoughts: (In this section, write down your final thoughts about lessons learned from this lesson and/or your exposure field trip.)

CHAPTER THREE
RELATIONSHIPS

"It takes teamwork to make the dream work!" John Maxwell

Nothing significant in this world has been done by one person alone. Despite what you may feel at times because of circumstances such as being raised by a single parent, being abandoned by friends when you needed them the most, being doubted by your teachers, or not making the team, these are not reasons to think you can do things on your own.

Christianity couldn't have spread like it has without the help of millions of disciples. World leaders such as Julius Caesar, Alexander the Great, and even evil leaders such as Adolph Hitler couldn't have accomplished what they did without the help of others who supported their dreams.

Think about your favorite sports teams. Tom Brady couldn't have won five Super Bowls without Coach Bill Belichick and his other teammates. Michael Jordan needed Scottie Pippen and Dennis Rodman to win his sixth basketball championship. And the Dallas Cowboys are becoming America's team again because of a great offensive line, including exciting young players like Dak Prescott, Ezekiel Elliott, and Dez Bryant.

Just like these leaders who have accomplished their dreams, you too need other people to help you achieve your dreams. The phrase "It takes teamwork to make the dream work," coined by John Maxwell, means that only by working with a team can individuals fulfill their dreams. Maxwell also said, "There are no lone rangers." In this chapter, we will learn about the crucial importance of the right relationships to move you forward in your career as well as in your personal life.

In the book's chapter "Born Sinner, Opposite of a Winner," by Ramon Harper, he wrote, "Despite my thinking as a teenager, I developed a keen sense of the value of relationships that has always been a key to my success. As an adult, I now understand that when you want to get something done, it isn't always what you know but who you know. When we conduct our D.R.E.A.M.S. seminars, we focus on relationships as a key aspect because those who understand the importance of relationships and are able to leverage them are able to achieve their goals without taking advantage of people."

Once you get to college—as we are certain that you will as a result of reading our book and completing this workbook—then you will experience fraternities or sororities and other organizations. These groups can provide great opportunities for you to build lifelong friendships that will benefit you in college and in your professional career.

Get involved in different types of organizations, whether at school, at church, and in sports. In these groups and teams, you can build great social skills, learn how to trust others, and develop better communication skills. As a young person, the benefits of joining such groups can help you get into the right college and obtain scholarships. Once you begin your career, your experiences in these groups could help you get the right job or start your own company, such as the members of TDI have done.

CASE STUDIES
TERRENCE HALL, TDI MEMBER

As far as my social life in school, I tended to be the student other children wanted to be around. From an early age, I learned how to be a good friend. For example, during recess one day, the school administrators were trying to find one of my classmates. When they couldn't find her, my teacher said, "Just find Terry Hall, and I'm quite sure she will be close by," and it was true!

Through my natural family, my church family, my Alpha brothers, and my TallaDallas brothers, I have shown and been shown love in ways that are hard to imagine. Being part of each of these unique families has taken me far from my humble beginnings as a youth to my nurturing as a man. I can only thank God for allowing me to experience such love and support.

From my days on ASU's campus to my work experiences, personally and professionally, I've been able to count on my families. My biological family raised me to be the best man I could be. My church family brought me up with the right morals that would carry me throughout life. When I decided to pledge Alpha, I knew my TallaDallas brothers supported my decision. When I took a job in Texas, I knew Marc had my back with a place to stay and whatever else I might need. If I needed financial help, I knew TallaDallas, along with my frat brothers, were there if they could help. They all supported me in my decision to start my own mentoring business and helped me in any way they could.

Terrence is a member of Alpha Phi Alpha Fraternity and is now an educator and an entrepreneur in Talladega, Alabama.

KEVIN DURANT

NBA superstar Kevin Durant decided to leave the Oklahoma City Thunder to join the Golden State Warriors. Why? In Oklahoma City, Durant was partnered with a great player in Russell Westbrook, and together they came close to winning the NBA championship. But they didn't win, so Durant decided to leave Oklahoma City to join the Warriors, a basketball superpower.

Durant said, "I am also at a point in my life where it is of equal importance to find an opportunity that encourages my evolution as a man: moving out of my comfort zone to a new city and community which offers the greatest potential for my contribution and personal growth."

In order to have a shot at wining the championship, Durant knew he would have to be part of a winning team. He would need to surround himself with other great players who had the same vision and goals.

It's the same for you if you want to achieve your dreams. Getting close is rarely good enough. Instead, surround yourself with a winning team, and you will have greater success.

Kevin has been awarded many MVP awards and won his first NBA championship with the Golden State Warriors in the 2016–2017 season. He is one of the highest paid players in the world and has done endorsements for Foot Locker and Nike. He is also known for his community philanthropy.

WORKBOOK

KEYS TO SUCCESS
After reading the case studies, what keys did you find in Terrence's and Kevin's stories that stood out to you?

PERSONAL EVALUATION
You might have heard the phrase "You can tell a lot about a person's future based on who they hang with today." Who are the important people in your life?

Make a list of your current friends, and beside their names list the benefits they bring to your life. Then list your friends' good qualities as well as their bad ones. If their bad qualities outweigh their good ones, or some of their qualities could hinder you from achieving your dream, then you need to remove these people from your circle. This doesn't mean that you have to stop talking to them every day, but you do need to stop hanging out with them. One day, they may do something that is going to get you in big trouble, thus keeping you from achieving success.

How will you apply this knowledge to your life?

Dreamer's Challenge: (In this section, write down your assignment from your facilitator.)

Closing Thoughts: (In this section, write down your final thoughts about lessons learned from this lesson and/or your exposure field trip.)

CHAPTER FOUR
EXECUTION

"Failing to plan is planning to fail." Benjamin Franklin

No matter how great your dreams are, if you aren't able to set goals and execute those goals, then you will never see your dreams come to pass. TDI sells a line of t-shirts that have the following lines on them: Dream – Work = Sleep. Dream + Work = Success. These shirts describe our philosophy on the need to put in the work, to execute, in order to be successful.

Think back to the example of the cake mix box in Chapter One. Although you see a picture of a cake on the front of the box, there are certain ingredients you will need to obtain and specific instructions you will need to follow in order to have the cake you want. That is why setting goals is important.

Even at a young age, you should have goals. If you are going to make an A on a test, then study. If you want to be recruited to play football or to run track, set goals that will help you to increase your speed in the 40-yard dash. But no matter how many goals you have, they have to be SMART goals.

- **S** – Specific: Target a specific area for improvement.
- **M** – Measurable: Evaluate your progress toward your goal.
- **A** – Agreed upon: Identify who will do specific tasks and who needs to help get those tasks completed.
- **R** – Realistic: State what results can realistically be achieved, given available resources.
- **T** – Time-related: Specify when individual steps toward your goals can be achieved.

CASE STUDIES
BRYANT SPENCER, TDI MEMBER

I was tops in my class, but I still ran into doubters—this time they were my teachers. They tried to encourage me to go to junior college or maybe a trade school so that I would have a better chance for success, but I guess one of my teachers did have a little faith in me. She said, "When I first met you, I didn't think that you would amount to a hill of beans. But now I believe that you can attend a four-year university." I wasn't sure what to make of her comment, so I looked at her awkwardly, thanked her, and walked away. I had a plan in place, and now it was time to execute the first phase.

As I prepared for college, I focused on my GPA, community service, and extracurricular activities. I knew that I was in no position to pay for college, so if I was going to attend, I had to get there by pursuing scholarships.

During my senior year, I spent many days and nights looking for scholarships. I worked with the school's guidance counselor to identify potential opportunities. He wasn't much help. I guess he didn't get those types of questions that often. I couldn't rely on my parents and grandparents to assist me with my journey. I was the first to go to college and had to figure it out on my own, which included figuring out what school to attend, how to apply, how to pay for it, and all the other steps in between. I attended a few college fairs, which were helpful.

I took a rudimentary approach to narrowing down colleges. First, I considered my financial situation, so I knew that I had to look for economical options. Second, I compared the distance from home. The school had to be within driving distance, but I didn't want to be too close to home. Third, I had to find out how much room and board would cost. Fourth, I had to look at out-of-state fees, which narrowed my search to in-state schools. Finally, I discovered that private schools limited my financial aid options, so they were out. I knew that I was going to need every bit of free money I could find.

Bryant Spencer graduated from Alabama State University with a degree in marketing. He also has an executive MBA from MIT, a top Ivy League university. Bryant is a retail executive for a Fortune 500 company.

JAY Z

Born Shawn Carter in New York City in December 1969, Jay Z grew up in Brooklyn's drug-infested Marcy Projects. He used rap as an escape, appearing for the first time on *Yo! MTV Raps* in 1989. After selling millions of records with his Roc-a-Fella label, Jay Z created his own clothing line and founded an entertainment company.

The rapper married popular singer and actress Beyoncé in 2008. Jay Z was the first guest on Oprah's *Master Class* show when she started OWN network in 2011. Some of his keys to success are:

- Grind harder than the next man.

- Set goals for yourself.

- Be true to yourself.

- Picture the pinnacle.

- You are in control.

For this lesson on goal-setting and execution, let's look a bit closer at how Jay Z achieved success.

Jay Z's first goal was to create an album that went gold. Everything he did was to lead him to reach that goal. Once he reached that goal, he set a new one: He wanted to show the rap world that an artist can become an executive in the music industry, so he became the CEO of Def Jam Records.

On the Billboard 200, Jay Z holds the record for most number one albums. He's a successful businessman and philanthropist. He's also been involved with various film and television projects.

Like Jay Z, be goal-oriented. Set clear, actionable goals for yourself. Once you have achieved them, then set new, bigger goals. Achieving your first goal will motivate you to climb the next mountain.

KEYS TO SUCCESS
After reading the case studies, what keys did you find in Bryan's and Jay Z's stories that stood out to you?

PERSONAL EVALUATION
How will you apply this knowledge to your life?

Dreamer's Challenge: (In this section, write down your assignment from your facilitator.)

Closing Thoughts: (In this section, write down your final thoughts about lessons learned from this lesson and/or your exposure field trip.)

CHAPTER FIVE
ATTITUDE

"It's Your ATTITUDE, not your APTITUDE that determines your ALTITUDE."
Zig Ziglar

Your attitude and your behavior are linked together like Facebook and Instagram. So when you look in the mirror, ask yourself the following questions:

- Are my beliefs and my behavior getting me where I want to go?

- Do people want to be around me?

- Am I a good friend?

- Am I a good sibling?

- Am I a great teammate?

- Do people want to hear what I have to say?

- Do I work well in groups?

Answering these questions will help you figure out if your attitude, behavior, and character are in check.

CASE STUDIES
TERRANCE TURNER, TDI MEMBER
When I was a senior in college, I applied for a job as an FBI intern in Washington, DC. But things didn't go so well for me because of a few character flaws I had.

The recruiter told me that there were a few details I would need to take care of before I could start my internship. Just protocol, she said. I had to get security clearance, and I would be asked general questions about whether I had any undisclosed items, if I had ill intent toward the US government, and if I had any drug use within the last two years.

Drug use? I had no idea I would be asked about that. I was never a big drug user, but I had tried smoking weed twice while hanging out at a couple of parties. But my brief dalliance with drugs had happened a year and a half before, and I hadn't done it since.

I didn't know what to do. Should I 'fess up and tell the truth, or should I take my chances with the lie detector test? I thought that maybe if I confessed what happened, they would understand and let me through. I was even less sure about how well I would do up against the lie detector. But I had to make it to DC. This was huge for me as well as for my family, and my parents had proudly told everyone we knew about the internship, so I couldn't let them down. I agonized over my dilemma for weeks.

On the day of the test, I still didn't know what I was going to do, but I finally decided to tell the agent the truth and hope for the best. It didn't work in my favor. Although the agent was sympathetic, the rule was clear.

I couldn't face my parents with the truth. I told them that I couldn't accept the internship because I had to take a summer class that wouldn't be offered again for several semesters and missing the class would keep me from graduating. None of that was true, but I had to come up with something. When they read our book, *It Was All a Dream*, they'll know the truth, so I should probably tell them before it comes out.

Looking back, I know now that I should have been man enough to tell my family the truth about not getting the internship back then, but this was a different type of fear. I didn't want to disappoint my parents, and I didn't want to struggle through trying to get them to understand. In retrospect, my parents would have understood even through their disappointment. The love of good parents is unconditional, and they will support you even after you mess up.

Despite this minor setback, Terrance learned from his mistakes and has since obtained his master's degree and become a Certified Public Accountant. He now serves as vice president at Emerson Retail Solutions (ERS) in Atlanta.

PRESIDENT BARACK OBAMA

Instead of turning a blind eye to the police-involved shooting deaths of several African American men during his final term, President Barack Obama organized a town hall meeting, which was shown on network television in July 2016. He was joined by a Howard University student, the Milwaukee, Wisconsin police chief, and several concerned parents and police officers.

The town hall forum gave everyday citizens an opportunity to address the President directly with their questions and concerns. The following ideas were affirmed during the discussion:

- All US citizens must take responsibility for their actions and treat everyone with respect.

- We must work together to discuss important topics and address problems nonviolently.

- We can't put the burden on the police alone.

- We must invest in our communities through education and public assistance.

One of the main takeaways from the recent tension in the United States is that attitude plays a huge part in how a person is treated and what rewards that person will experience. There will be countless times when you'll be faced with situations where "taking the high road" is the best option. Maintaining your reputation and credibility is worth it.

It's not a sign of weakness to humble yourself to respect and to accept someone else's thought, point, or position. Therefore, always try to listen intently, and assume positive intent until shown otherwise. Most importantly, attitude is everything, so pick a good one!

President Obama left office in January 2017 but has remained active in the public eye. In March 2017, he was awarded the Profile in Courage Award from the John F. Kennedy Presidential Library and Museum. He has given speeches internationally as well as in the United States.

KEYS TO SUCCESS
After reading the case studies, what keys did you find in Terrance's and President Obama's stories that stood out to you?

PERSONAL EVALUATION
How will you apply this to your life?

Dreamer's Challenge: (In this section, write down your assignment from your facilitator.)

Closing Thoughts: (In this section, write down your final thoughts about lessons learned from this lesson and/or your exposure field trip.)

CHAPTER SIX
MOTIVATION

"If you are working on something that you really care about, you don't have to be pushed. The vision pulls you." Steve Jobs

In our book, *It Was All a Dream*, TDI member Herman Moncrief said, "As I sit and gather my thoughts to document my brief life up to this moment, there's one word that resonates with me being in the place that I am in today: *choice*. A choice is an act of selecting or making a decision when faced with two or more possibilities. Having the ability to make a decision, good or bad, is paramount to being alive.

In my opinion, there is nothing more defeating than not having the ability to choose. Whether you are choosing between good or bad, right or wrong, left or right, you have the ability to choose, and that ability to make a choice is powerful. It's no coincidence that the adjectives of the word *choice* are ones that indicate the best (*excellent, exclusive, prime, exquisite, precious, rare*). So the word *choice* is sacred to me, and I continue to put myself in situations that afford me the ability to choose.

If you are going to choose, choose to be great, choose to make an impact, choose to become a leader of men, and above all else choose situations that continually allow you to have a CHOICE. In order to achieve your dreams, you have to be self-motivated. You can't expect someone else to inspire you or motivate you to want to be great. For me, having the ability to choose was and is my greatest motivation along with my dreams."

CASE STUDIES
HERMAN MONCRIEF, TDI MEMBER

My chapter in our book, *It Was All a Dream*, is entitled "Now My Whole Crew Is Loungin', No More Public Housin'." That should give you a bit more insight into my motivation.

When I was living back in Prattville, Alabama, I got another 9-to-5 at a plant that manufactured brake pads. Initially, I began working the graveyard shift and was soon promoted to the first shift. My uncle worked at the same plant and had been employed there for many years. Once I moved to the first shift, I rode to work with him every day, which was the perfect situation for me.

I worked at the plant with my uncle for over a year. Each day, I would take my lunch break with him and some of the other guys who had been employed there for over 20 years. Our lunches consisted of leftovers from the previous night's meal or potted meat, crackers, and a warm honey bun (can't forget the honey bun). Our lunchtime conversations were always entertaining, and I enjoyed working with those guys. But I began to wonder if there was anything else out there for me. The guys would tell me to do more with my life, and I would always listen, but I had no idea what more I could do.

The work at the plant was easy. I worked on a rotary saw, and my job was to cut the brake shoes into sections so they could fit onto the 18-wheelers. Working conditions weren't that great. It was incredibly hot inside the plant and dusty. At the end of each shift, you could blow your nose for hours, and black residue from the dust in the air would come out on the tissue.

One morning, I arrived at work at my normal time; but when I got to the front entrance, I knew something was different. There were people sitting outside at the picnic tables looking dejected. My first thought was that there had been an accident and that someone had been hurt or, even worse, killed. Later, we found out that the company had executed a large layoff, which affected the entire third shift and a number of people on the second shift.

For the moment, it didn't appear that my job was affected at all, so I proceeded to my workstation and began my day. Midway through my shift, the assistant plant manager told me that due to a slow-down in business, a decision was made to eliminate some shifts, which affected several jobs. He assured me that my job was safe, but he needed me to move to the second shift. Initially, I thought I was lucky to have a job, so I thanked him for the continued employment and accepted the spot on the second shift.

But I realized that I was comfortable with my situation on first shift, and my life was organized around those hours. I rode to work with my uncle, and he was going to continue to work first shift, so moving to a later shift wasn't the move for me. I returned to the plant manager's office and let him know that I no longer wanted to move to second shift and that first shift was a better fit for me. He looked at me and politely said, "Herman, you do not have a choice."

I will never forget how I felt when he said that to me. Here I was, 21 years old, and I was being told I didn't have a choice. I managed to get through most of my workday, but for some reason I could not get that statement out of my head. It was eating at me, and I asked myself, *If I have no choice this early in life, what does the future hold for me?*

I turned off my machine, cleaned up my workstation, and walked back to the manager's office. I took off my hardhat and safety glasses and looked him in the eye and said, "I just wanted to let you know that I do have a choice, and I choose to leave effective immediately."

Given that the shift hadn't ended, I sat outside until my uncle finished his shift. Before the shift ended, I was summoned to come back into the building because the head plant manager wanted to speak with me. He told me he liked my work product and offered to retain my position on the first shift, but making the choice to leave and control my own destiny empowered me like never before. It was at that moment I made the decision to further my education and do so with the same vigor and aggressiveness I had once done as an athlete.

After obtaining his degree from Alabama State University, Herman became a Certified Public Accountant (CPA) and has started his own CPA practice in Nashville, Tennessee.

KHALED KHALED

Khaled Khaled, better known as DJ Khaled, is also a social media superstar with his motivational Snapchats and Instagram posts. If you aren't following him @djkhaled, then you are missing out. He is the ultimate self-motivator, and he inspires the world with his "Major Keys to Success."

Some of those keys are:

- "They don't want you to win."

- "Watch your back, but, more importantly, when you get out of the shower, dry your back. It's a cold world out there."

- "Be a star. Be a superstar."

- "I remember when I ain't have no jacuzzi."

- "All I do is win, win, win no matter what."

- "The other day, the grass was brown. Now its green cuz I ain't give up. Never surrender."

- "When you stop making excuses and you work hard and go hard, you will be very successful."

- "They'll try to close the door on you. Just open it!"

- "We have to get money. We have no choice. It cost money to eat."

- "Almond milk + cinnamon crunch = major key to success!"

These are just of few of his motivational quotes. But when you study his life, you will see how this New Orleans native born to Palestinian parents went from working at a local radio store, where he met Birdman and Lil Wayne, to becoming a DJ to producing major hit records to becoming the major celebrity he is today. The keys to DJ's success come from his motivation, which turns his dreams into reality.

DJ Khaled is a record producer, radio personality, DJ, record label executive, and author.

KEYS TO SUCCESS
After reading the case studies, what keys did you find in Herman's and Khaled's stories that stood out to you?

PERSONAL EVALUATION
How will you apply this knowledge to your life?

Dreamer's Challenge: (In this section, write down your assignment from your facilitator.)

Closing Thoughts: (In this section, write down your final thoughts about lessons learned from this lesson and/or your exposure field trip.)

CHAPTER SEVEN
SACRIFICE

"The best way to find yourself is to lose yourself in the service of others."
Mahatma Gandhi

There will be times when you must help other people and not expect anything in return. Instead, your benefit is knowing that the person you helped has overcome some hardship or succeeded in their goal or mission.

In our D.R.E.A.M.S. seminars, we discuss how "it's OK to be king-maker sometimes." Being selfless is a character trait that will be valued by everyone in your life: parents, siblings, friends, classmates, teachers, coaches, mentors, co-workers, community leaders, and your employees (if you become a business owner). When you sacrifice your time, God-given gifts or talents, energy, and money, we are confident that one day you will benefit from the sacrifice of someone else, even if it's someone you have never met.

CASE STUDIES
TDI MEMBERS

In *It Was All a Dream*, several founding TDI members talk about how they grew up in single-parent homes. The sacrifices our mothers or fathers made throughout our upbringing are not the only factors that made us successful men. Part of what has motivated us is starting the Turning Dreams Into Realities Scholarship & Mentorship Program. Through our service to young people, it is our hope that they will not only benefit from being more prepared for business and life but also moved to help others that come after them.

By now, you should have finished reading *It Was All a Dream*. Your next assignment is to choose one of the book authors to whom you most closely relate, and use his life as your case study in this section and to answer the questions below.

THURGOOD MARSHALL

Thurgood Marshall was the first black justice on the United States Supreme Court. But he was also an important figure in the Civil Rights Movement.

Marshall was born on July 2, 1908 in Baltimore, Maryland, the great-grandson of a slave. He graduated from Lincoln University in Oxford, Pennsylvania, the first degree-issuing Historically

Black College. After graduating, Marshall applied to the University of Maryland Law School but wasn't admitted because of his race. This denial, however, would help change the trajectory of his life. He was later admitted to Howard University Law School and graduated in 1933, first in his class.

One of the main priorities that Dean Charles Hamilton Houston laid out for his law students was the overturning of *Plessy v. Ferguson*, which allowed segregation based on the principle of separate but equal. Marshall argued the case of Donald Gaines Murray, a black Amherst College graduate who had also been denied admission to the University of Maryland Law School.

In 1936, Marshall opened a private practice but also worked for the National Association for the Advancement of Colored People (NAACP). He argued 32 cases in front of the US Supreme Court, the most famous being *Brown v. Board of Education of Topeka*, the case that ended legal segregation within the United States. In all, Marshall won 29 of the 32 cases he argued in front of the court.

President Lyndon B. Johnson nominated Thurgood Marshall to the United States Supreme Court in June 1967, and Marshall served on the court for 24 years. Today, there are many monuments to Marshall's memory, including Baltimore International Thurgood Marshall Airport.

KEYS TO SUCCESS
After reading the case studies, what keys did you find in the stories of the TDI members and Thurgood Marshall that stood out to you?

PERSONAL EVALUATION
How will you apply this knowledge to your life?

Dreamer's Challenge: (In this section, write down your assignment from your facilitator.)

Closing Thoughts: (In this section, write down your final thoughts about lessons learned from this lesson and/or your exposure field trip.)

CONCLUSION

If you can dream it, you can make it happen. We did!

We hope that you enjoyed this resource and that it helped you to discover your dreams and gave you practical tools to turn them into reality. After over 20 years, the members of TDI have grown as men, fathers, and professionals. We have overcome various trials and challenges just like you have, and we have used some common principles that helped us to succeed. The key to our success was our D.R.E.A.M.S. (Discipline, Relationships, Execution, Attitude, Motivation, and Sacrifice).

Our goal for creating this resource was to help you identify ways to see the journey of life through a broader lens. In addition to our life stories, we included stories of men who are culturally relevant so that you could learn from their successes and failures, too.

From athletes such as Trent Richardson and Kevin Durant, to entertainers such as DJ Khaled and Jay Z, all the way to world-changers such as President Barack Obama and Justice Thurgood Marshall—all of these men had dreams. Some achieved theirs, and others had to overcome various challenges, but you can see the D.R.E.A.M.S. principles woven into their stories.

Whether you were part of a group mentor program at your church, community organization, or school, we hope our book, *It Was All a Dream*, as well as this workbook, have benefited you in some way. As you finish high school and prepare for college, we would love to hear your story. And if you would like to be part of our college scholarship and mentor program, please visit us at www.tdi2r.org.

ABOUT THE AUTHORS
DR. BRENCLEVETON "DONTA" TRUSS

Brencleveton "Donta" Truss was born in Atlanta, Georgia, but grew up in Talladega, Alabama. He graduated from Alabama State University, where he received a bachelor's degree, a master's degree, and a doctorate in Educational Leadership, Policy and Law.

Dr. Truss is the author of *Innovation in Higher Education: An Analysis of Organizational Change and Its Role in Retaining Students*. He is involved in community activities and was the president of the Cuthbert, Georgia Rotary Club, and he is a proud member of Kappa Alpha Psi Fraternity, Inc.

Recently, Dr. Truss was selected and honored as one of the "Best and the Brightest: Top Forty Under Forty Persons" in the state of Georgia by *Georgia Trend Magazine*. He is the associate vice president for institutional research, planning, and effectiveness at The Fort Valley State University and is the CEO of Resource One, LLC, which is a consulting firm that focuses on helping organizations grow and operate at their most optimal level. Additionally, Resource One, LLC provides grant-writing services and professional development for many educational and non-educational non-profit agencies.

On July 2, 2006, Dr. Truss became a licensed minister, and he is a proud husband and a busy father.

RAMONE HARPER

Ramone is the founder of BNB Consulting and Associates, a management and consulting firm that contracts with ministries, major corporations, not-for-profits, and start-ups in the areas of business organization and development, staff and leadership development, and branding. He also serves as executive pastor at Kingdom Church in Ewing, New Jersey.

Ramone earned his BS in public relations with a minor in business administration from Alabama State University, where he graduated summa cum laude in 1997. He is currently enrolled at Regents University, working on his masters of divinity degree. Recently, he was selected as one of the "Ebony Men of the Year" by the Alpha Kappa Alpha Sorority, Inc., included in the 2013-2015 *Who's Who in Black Houston* publication as one of the top entrepreneurs, and honored as one of Houston's "Top 50 Entrepreneurs" in 2015.

Originally from Detroit, Michigan, Ramone lived the majority of his teenage years in the Dallas-Fort Worth area. He is married to his life partner, Verily, and they have four children and one grandchild.

BRYANT SPENCER

Bryant Spencer is a retail executive with over 18 years of merchandising and marketing experience, including strategic planning, budgeting, forecasting, and financial analysis. He is experienced in product development and private label and international brands.

Bryant grew up in Carrollton, Alabama. He graduated from Alabama State University with a BS in marketing and is obtaining his MBA from Massachusetts Institute of Technology (MIT). He is a recipient of numerous professional awards, and he completed several business development courses from Northwestern's Kellogg School of Management, Notre Dame's Mendoza College of Business, and DePaul University. Bryant and his wife, Melanie, live in Rhode Island.

MARC P. DESGRAVES IV, CPA

Marc is a Certified Public Accountant with a wealth of diversified experience over multiple decades, including tax preparation, business formation and start-up services, mergers and acquisitions, Sarbanes-Oxley compliance, risk assessment, forensic accounting, internal audit, and big four external audit. He currently continues to serve the public through his CPA practice, Desgraves CPA.

Marc is proud of his civic contributions, which include providing tax services on a pro bono basis as well as volunteering his time through organizations such as the National Association of Black Accountants and serving on the board of directors for charter schools.

In his personal time, Marc enjoys playing basketball, tackling home projects, and mentoring young people through organizations such as Big Brothers Big Sisters or coaching youth sports.

TYRISH GARRETT

Tyrish Garrett was born in Talladega, Alabama, the son of Brenda Garrett and Howard Leonard. He received a BS in marketing from Alabama State University and his MBA in business administration from Troy State University.

For 16 years, Tyrish has been employed by United Parcel Service, where he has worked as the sales/marketing supervisor for the last five years. He is responsible for implementation of sales strategies, evaluation of customer compliance and value, and cross-functional support for profitable sales growth. Previously, he was a finance supervisor and was responsible for district profitability analysis, customer profitability, and auditor training.

Tyrish has served as a volunteer for United Way, where he met with company coordinators to plan, organize, and schedule employee meetings and assist with developing campaign goals.

TERRENCE HALL

Terrence Hall is originally from Talladega, Alabama. He enrolled at Alabama State University in the fall of 1993 and majored in business administration, with a concentration in finance. After college, Terrence worked as a loan processor for Northeastern Financial Services and as a loan officer for Regions Financial Corporation.

Terrence then was employed by Delta Airlines, where he worked in global sales support and services. He later worked as a learning support trainer and traveled extensively, domestically and internationally, to implement new policies and procedures to employees. He was awarded with the Certificate of Excellence for outstanding performance; was a four-time member of the renowned Pinnacle Club; and was a nominee for the Chairman's Club, which is the highest award for a Delta Airlines employee.

Presently, Terrence works with his tutorial service, F.I.N.A.O. (Failure Is Not An Option), through which he mentors youth of all ages and encourages them to make good grades. He's also an independent business owner of Total Life Changes, a health and wellness organization.

Terrence is a member of Shady Grove Baptist Church, where he serves as a Crusaders counselor. He is currently in a relationship and is a renowned member of Alpha Phi Alpha Fraternity, Inc.

TERRANCE TURNER, CPA

Terrance is from Talladega, Alabama. He graduated summa cum laude from ASU in 1997 with a BS in accounting. He then graduated from the University of Arkansas with a master's in business administration.

Starting his career at the Dallas office of Arthur Andersen as an auditor, Terrance later accepted a position in Atlanta, Georgia, in Arthur Andersen's Transactions Advisory Services (M&A). After leaving Andersen, he accepted a position as a financial controller for a business within the Emerson Climate Technologies Retail Solutions Division (ERS) in 2002. He was later promoted to director of finance, director of operations, and director of strategic planning; and he currently serves as vice president.

Terrance has been married for 12 years to his wife, Kerri, and they live in the Atlanta metro area. They have two boys, Jackson (9) and Xavier (7).

DR. ANTHONY LEWIS

Dr. Anthony Lewis is from Talladega, Alabama. He is married to Tiffany, and they are the proud parents of six children (Jasmine, Akirah, Anthony II, Sierra, Kailey, and Braxton). He received a BS and a MEd in Special Education from Alabama State University, as well as a certification in educational leadership. He received a PhD in educational leadership and policy analysis from the University of Missouri.

Dr. Lewis began his career as a special education teacher at Jefferson Davis High School in Montgomery, Alabama, where he taught for six years. He was later appointed assistant principal and then principal at E. D. Nixon Elementary School in Montgomery.

Because of his successes as principal, he was recruited to work with the Kansas City public school system in Missouri, where he currently works as director of elementary schools in the department of school leadership. In this position, Dr. Lewis provides leadership for elementary principals, schools, and programs; oversees school planning, implementation, coordination, and evaluation of elementary schools; and ensures that program activities comply with district policies and state statutes.

HERMAN MONCRIEF, CPA

Herman is originally from Prattville, Alabama, and currently resides in Spring Hill, Tennessee. He is married to April and is the proud parent of fraternal twins, Asia and Bryce.

In 1997, Herman received a BS degree from Alabama State University, with a concentration in accounting, and he is a certified public accountant in Georgia. Shortly after graduation from ASU, he relocated to Atlanta, Georgia, and began his professional career as a staff accountant for The Maxim Group. He has served as staff and senior auditor for Arthur Andersen, corporate controller for InterCept, Inc., audit manager for KPMG LLP in Atlanta, and corporate controller and principal accounting officer of American Software, Inc. (NASDAQ:AMSWA). American Software is a publicly traded software company operating primarily in the Enterprise Resource Planning (ERP) and Supply Chain segments of the software industry.

Herman previously served as the vice president of finance for MEDHOST, Inc., where he was responsible for all aspects of accounting and financial reporting, in addition to managing and directing the general accounting, billing, credit, collections, and tax functions of the company. He now runs his own accounting practice and serves on the boards of Turning Dreams Into Realties (TDI) and the United Way of Williamson County.

JEREMY SPRATLING

Jeremy L. Spratling was born and raised in Talladega, Alabama. In 1996, he graduated from Auburn University at Montgomery with a BS in economics. He graduated from the Graduate School of Banking at Louisiana State University in 2004.

Jeremy worked in the financial services industry for 14 years before founding Corporate Facilities Management, Inc. He handles the day-to-day operations and management.

Jeremy is married to Freddie, and they have an active daughter and a son. Jeremy enjoys fishing, reading, physical activity, and community involvement. He also mentors youth, business owners, and aspiring entrepreneurs.

DEMETRICE JONES

Demetrice A. Jones attended Alabama State University (ASU) in 1993 and earned his bachelor of science degree in criminal justice. In 2003, he enrolled in the ASU graduate program and received his master of science degree in general counseling. Demetrice is CEO of Clear Path Youth and Family Services, LLC, which is located in Montgomery, Alabama. His agency provides counseling services for at-risk youths who have encountered personal, family, and behavioral issues at home, in their communities, and at school. He also serves on the management team at a local financial institution.

Demetrice has written and published two relationship novels, *When the Truth Is Revealed* (2008) and *If He Won't, I Will* (2009). He is currently working on his third novel, *Now That the Truth Is Revealed*.

WAYS TO SUPPORT TDI
SUPPORT OUR MISSION

Book our D.R.E.A.M.S. Professional Development Seminar for your next event, tailored to motivate and inspire professionals to achieve their dreams.

Consider partnering with us by making a tax-deductible contribution. Your donation will go toward the awarding of collegiate scholarships for the upcoming school year. If you are interested in being a partner of our organization, please make checks payable to TDI, Turning Dreams Into Realities, and send donations to PO Box 270933, Flower Mound, Texas 75027-0933. Or you can donate through our secure online PayPal account at www.tdi2r.org.

Should you need additional information, do not hesitate to e-mail us at info@tdi2r.org. Thank you in advance for your support.

Connect With TDI

Mailing Address
T.D.I.
PO Box 270933
Flower Mound, TX 75027-0933

E-mail
info@tdi2r.org

Website
www.tdi2r.org

Facebook
www.tdi2r.org

Twitter
@turningdreams

Instagram
@tdi_inc

ADDITIONAL NOTES

WORKBOOK

WORKBOOK

WORKBOOK

WORKBOOK